Herman Baker
President 1939–1987

Richard Baker
President 1987–1997

Dwight Baker
President 1997–present

THE
Baker Book House
STORY

Ann Byle

BakerBooks

a division of Baker Publishing Group
Grand Rapids, Michigan

© 2014 by Baker Publishing Group

Published by Baker Books
a division of Baker Publishing Group
P.O. Box 6287, Grand Rapids, MI 49516-6287
www.bakerbooks.com

Printed in the United States of America

ISBN 978-0-8010-1658-5

Our mission is to publish high-quality writings that represent historic Christianity and serve the diverse interests and concerns of evangelical readers.

Contents

Sidebars

Welcome

In the fall of 1987 our freshly appointed president, Richard Baker, gathered together a team of his key leaders to discuss the publishing company that was now under his care. Although I was anything but a leader at the time, he graciously invited me to participate in the crafting of a company mission statement. Although Richard does not tend toward formalities, he recognized the significance of a statement that accurately reflected our history and would guide our publishing activities in the future. Over the course of many sessions, our conversations were distilled into one concise statement, and then, with our stated mission in hand, we all returned to our respective tasks and got down to business.

Twenty years later a few of us revisited the original mission statement to evaluate its durability and refine some terms. The meeting required hardly an hour. We were impressed to discover that our statement required no significant alterations, even after two decades of perpetual transitions in the publishing profession. This continuity is one of the great blessings of serving the church with fine writings, even as the ground shifts beneath us.

> Our mission is to publish high-quality writings that represent historic Christianity and serve the diverse interests and concerns of evangelical readers.

This year, in celebration of our seventy-five years of fidelity to this mission, we welcome our companions to explore a history of the kingdom activities of Baker Book House Company. To borrow a line from our founder, Herman Baker, this is the best business to be in. Today Herman's observation is more accurate than ever.

Dwight Baker
CEO/President
Baker Book House Company

1 The Early Years
1939–1949

Herman Baker was fourteen years old when he and his family emigrated from the Zoutkamp area in the northern region of the Netherlands. The oldest son of Ricco (Richard) Bakker and Jenny Kregel Bakker had been born in the United States, but his family had returned to their homeland when he was two years old.

In 1925, when the family made its way again to Ellis Island and then by train to Grand Rapids, Michigan, they were here to stay. They quickly made a home in the Dutch community that had grown steadily in Grand Rapids and West Michigan since 1847, when the first immigrants arrived. The Bakker family dropped the second "k" from its name when Ricco became a United States citizen a number of years later.

For Herman, the Dutch language was familiar in the neighborhoods around Eastern Avenue and Franklin Street. The Reformed faith of the immigrants was preached in the churches and fiercely defended and openly discussed in the workplaces and homes of a people who often read theology in their free time.

Shortly after arriving in Grand Rapids, young Herman found a job working part-time in the bookstore owned by his uncle, Louis Kregel (brother of his mother, Jenny). Those days working in the bookstore fueled Herman's love for religious classics and jump-started his dream of beginning a book business of his own.

Inspection room, Ellis Island, New York. From Ellis Island, Ricco Bakker's family traveled by train to Grand Rapids, Michigan.

Immigrants awaiting examination, Ellis Island

Before Herman fulfilled that dream, he had other business to attend to. He and Angeline Sterkenberg married in 1932 and began their family. First Joanne was born, and then Richard in 1935. Ruth Ellen and Peter joined the family in the next years.

At age twenty-eight, with help from his in-laws, Herman Baker opened his bookstore at 1019 Wealthy Street in Grand Rapids. The year was 1939—the Great Depression was nearing its end and German troops invaded Poland in the opening salvos of World War II. Herman paid just eighteen dollars a month to rent the bookstore space, which he filled with homemade shelves that displayed almost five hundred used books he had collected over the years. His equipment consisted of two used desks and a typewriter purchased at the Salvation Army.

Herman Baker, four years after arriving in Grand Rapids from the Netherlands, poses at the Eastern Avenue Christian Reformed Church picnic in 1929.

The demand for used religious books soon exceeded expectations. Herman expanded his business into several ground-floor rooms and then into the basement. Continued growth meant purchasing adjoining buildings and converting upstairs apartments into storage and display rooms.

Just a year passed after opening the store before Herman Baker took his first steps into publishing books. In 1940 Baker Book House released *More Than Conquerors: An Interpretation of the Book of Revelation* by Dr. William Hendriksen, professor of New

Testament exegetical theology at Calvin Seminary, located a short distance from the store.

More Than Conquerors proved to be the sort of title Baker loved to publish: conservative, scholarly, biblical, and timeless. The book is still in print and continues to gather praise nearly seventy-five years after the original publication.

Herman Baker purchased the Wealthy Street building in 1942, gradually growing the business through the war years. There were times, however, when he had to wait for money to come in before buying postage stamps to send out more catalogs. The catalogs were painstakingly typed by hand, with workers going through every book on the shelves and listing author, title, and price. Buyers sent back their order form with payment, and staff

> *More Than Conquerors: An Interpretation of the Book of Revelation* was the first book published by Baker Book House. It released in 1940, just a year after Herman Baker started his business.

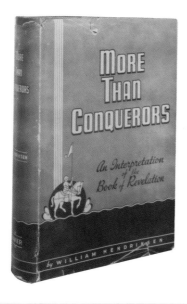 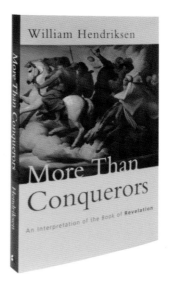

pulled the books from the shelves and mailed them out. The war years saw the first new and used fiction sold at the store, in part to draw in the many women who stayed home while the men went off to war.

The only "printing" machine Baker Book House ever owned was a 1946 A. B. Dick mimeograph. Shown here are Ben Veldkamp cranking the mimeograph and Edwin Oppenhuizen collecting the sheets.

This early photo of Baker Book House was taken during the holiday season. The apartments were still in use on the second floor, and no sign was yet attached above the building.

Baker knew how to sell books. As the tenth anniversary of the business approached, he and his staff came up with the novel idea of reissuing the popular *Barnes' Notes*, a commentary series that had already been a bestseller for over a century. Its last reissue was in 1852. But reissuing the twenty volumes would cost a prohibitive $30,000 for two thousand printed and bound sets. Herman didn't have that kind of capital, but he did have a salesman's instincts. Beginning in early 1949, Baker Book House issued the series on the Volume-a-Month Plan at three dollars per book, a plan "that

Publishing in West Michigan

Grand Rapids was home to a large Dutch population that loved to read. Herman Baker was one of several entrepreneurs who began selling and publishing books. Louis Kregel, Herman's uncle, started Kregel Books in 1909 by importing Dutch-language religious books and selling them from his home. He soon opened a bookstore and also began selling used religious books. Louis's son Robert Kregel took over upon Louis's death, and in 1949 the business expanded to include publication of reprints of religious classics. It is now called Kregel Publications.

William B. Eerdmans Sr. was the son of a Dutch textile manufacturer who immigrated to Grand Rapids in 1902. In 1911 Eerdmans and Brant Sevensma formed the Eerdmans-Sevensma Company, specializing in theological textbooks. By 1915 Eerdmans was sole owner of the William B. Eerdmans Publishing Company, specializing in its early years in books relating to John Calvin. Bill Eerdmans Jr. is the current president, only the second in the company's history.

Brothers Peter and Bernard Zondervan, nephews of William Eerdmans Sr., founded their company, Zondervan, in nearby Grandville, Michigan, in 1931. Zondervan's first book, *Women of the Old Testament*, was published in 1933. The company is now part of HarperCollins Christian Publishing.

Herman Baker corresponded regularly with these men through the years—and the four companies remain friendly competitors to this day.

Earliest employees, from left: Herman Baker; Ben Veldkamp, accountant and business manager, hired full-time in 1947; Clarence Dykhouse, sales and promotion manager, hired in 1941; Cornelius Zylstra, editor of the publication program, hired in 1949.

has proved very popular with purchasers of modest means," according to the tenth-anniversary catalog. More than twenty thousand volumes were ordered in just five months.

Description of *Barnes' Notes* from the tenth-anniversary catalog: "The form in which this Bible commentary now appears has been the subject of general admiration. The complete set consists of twenty handsome, gray, matching volumes. The title is attractively stamped in gold on a field of red on the back of each book. Everyone agrees that the set has eye appeal."

The Volume-a-Month Plan for *Barnes' Notes* was one of Herman Baker's most successful bookselling innovations.

By 1949 Baker Book House was among the largest distributors of new and used religious books in the United States and abroad. Orders came from as close as the next block to as far away as South Africa, Korea, and Hungary.

2 Years of Change
1950–1964

The years following the end of World War II in 1945 brought growth across America, especially, thanks to the GI Bill, at colleges and universities. Seminaries and Bible colleges expanded as well and soon found themselves in need of reference works, commentaries, textbooks, and preaching aids. They sought books on archaeology, Christian education, church history, and a host of other topics. Baker Book House was poised to answer that need thanks to its newly minted publishing program, its deep inventory of used books, and improvements in the offset printing process that made reprints easier to produce.

The next major project after *Barnes' Notes* was reprinting the thirteen-volume *New Schaff-Herzog Encyclopedia of Religious Knowledge*—another Volume-a-Month promotion—and adding in 1955 a two-volume supplement, the *Twentieth Century Encyclopedia of Religious Knowledge*.

The early 1950s were years of change for Baker Book House and the Christian publishing world in general. The Wealthy Street store

Baker Book House, located at 1019 Wealthy Street, after a 1953 remodel. The original store grew to include upstairs rooms and additional ground-floor space. Publishing offices and the bookstore still shared the same building.

underwent a complete renovation inside and out in 1953, providing additional space and improvements for both publishing division office staff and the bookstore. New books and products were located on the first floor, with used books housed on the second floor.

Many of the bookstore employees came from nearby Calvin College. One of the most notable was Nicholas Wolterstorff, who taught for thirty years at Calvin College and has become a well-known author, philosopher, and theologian. He is currently the Noah Porter Professor Emeritus of Philosophical Theology at Yale University.

In the larger Christian publishing world, the Christian Booksellers Association (CBA) was incorporated in 1950 in Illinois with 219 charter member stores and offices at Moody Press. CBA held its first annual convention at the LaSalle Hotel in Chicago.

Baker Book House was a charter member of CBA and proudly displayed its wares in the convention hall at the 1950 event. In 1959 CBA came to Grand Rapids. Another remodel meant that visiting booksellers saw the best of Baker Book House when they toured the facilities as part of the convention activities.

Attendees of the 1959 CBA convention took buses to Baker Book House in order to tour the facilities. Here they stand in line outside the newly remodeled store.

In May 1959 Herman Baker wrote an article titled "So You Want to Write a Book" for the National Association of Evangelicals' magazine *United Evangelical Action*. The National Association of Evangelicals (NAE) had been founded in April 1942 in St. Louis in an effort to bring the until-then-fragmented evangelical, conservative churches across the country together as one voice. The NAE formed the National Religious Broadcasters (NRB) in 1944. Both the NRB and the NAE are still in existence today.

Baker Book House celebrated its twenty-fifth anniversary in 1964. The company created several new projects for the occasion, including a special in which buyers could get a free book with orders of ten dollars or more. The celebration also featured a manuscript contest, with the winning author receiving an expense-paid trip to the Holy Land.

The twenty-fifth-anniversary brochure announced several new publications to mark the occasion: *The Biblical World: A Dictionary of Biblical Archaeology*, edited by Charles F. Pfeiffer; the first in the new Baker Missionary Visuograms series, a set of forty flashcards on the life of William Carey, accompanied by a booklet with the story; and nearly fifty titles to be released in the fall of 1964. Backlist titles remained strong, including *Cruden's Unabridged Concordance* and *Principles of Biblical Interpretation* by Grand Rapids theologian Dr. Louis Berkhof. Other authors included Carl F. H. Henry, Ralph Earle, and William Hendriksen, author of *More Than Conquerors*.

Herman Baker stands between his two sons, Peter, left, and Richard, right.

By the twenty-fifth year, Herman Baker's sons, Richard and Peter, were part of the staff. Richard came on in 1957 after attending Calvin College

Excerpts from "So You Want to Write a Book" by Herman Baker

So you want to write a book. This is welcome news.

Evangelicals have a weighty responsibility. God has given man the task of studying His revelation, both special and general. We can be of great help to each other and to those beyond our circles by sharing the results of our research and thinking by means of the printed page. So you are to be congratulated on this desire. . . .

If evangelicalism is to hold its own or to regain ground, it will have to hold to the faith without wavering. But it will have to do more. Its scholarship will have to match or surpass that of those who have forsaken the faith. With those two qualifications the evangelical has a tremendous advantage. The liberal—if we may still use the term—speaks haltingly, hesitatingly, and with uncertainty. The evangelical can speak confidently, positively, and with conviction. I am pleased that you have reached the decision to grasp this opportunity. . . .

[Mr. Baker suggested these criteria for potential authors:]

1. Be sure your motivation is right.
2. Be sure the subject of your proposed book is worthwhile.
3. Be sure you are qualified to make a contribution.
4. Be sure you can express yourself effectively through the medium of the printed page. . . .

Are you still with me? If you have given up already as a result of this article, nothing is lost. You would have fallen by the wayside anyway. You can thank me for saving you time and effort.

If you still want to write a book, there is hope that you may become a powerful and positive influence in the interest of evangelical Christianity.

May God give you strength and wisdom. We are expecting great things from you. (*United Evangelical Action*, May 1959, pages 5 and 23)

and graduating from the Publishing Procedures Course sponsored by Radcliffe College. He worked in sales and promotion, covering the eastern territory. Peter joined the business after attending Calvin College and Davenport Business Institute. He visited Baker Book House accounts in the Midwest territory.

The used-book division of Baker Book House was an essential part of the business—Herman Baker, after all, began his profession as a dealer of used books—and accounted for a large share of its business. Gary Popma, who joined Baker Book House in 1959, helped purchase libraries, classify and shelve books, keep track of the stock, and oversee preparation of the used-book catalogs sent out several times a year. Along with used books, the division also sold out-of-print books.

"I went with Mr. Baker on book-buying trips," recalls Popma, who retired in 2004. "He had a heavy foot; I remember riding with him in his 1964 Limited Edition Buick Electra and smoking cigars. He loved a good pipe too. One time he hit something in the road that badly damaged the car. He ended up buying a new one exactly like it."

Popma, with help from employees such as Pat Reurink Hoeksema, who began working at Baker in 1961, kept the used-book section neat and well organized. Hoeksema and others typed each catalog by hand, moving a portable table and typewriter along the rows to document each book. Catalog pages were laid on light boards for proofreading. Once the catalogs were mailed out, employees had about two

Gary Popma and Pat Reurink Hoeksema kept the used-book division of Baker Book House in good working order. Hoeksema recalls, "Mr. Baker was a brilliant man. He knew every book on the shelves. He'd say, 'That book is on shelf one or two, about ten books down.'"

Richard Baker
Remembers

Richard Baker calls Baker Book House "the only job I ever had." He remembers many hours spent at 1019 Wealthy Street as a child and young adult, always doing something for the store. "My dad would say, 'Put those books in canonical order' or 'Put those books in alphabetical order,'" Rich recalls. "I got really good at that." He occasionally traveled with his dad visiting bookstores and searching out libraries to purchase before getting his own sales route when he was hired as a full-time employee in 1957.

Richard and his wife, Fran, married in 1957, and she occasionally traveled with him on sales trips. Later on, their older children, Dawn and Dwight, came along as well.

"I remember one thing my dad used to say that has stuck with me," Rich said. "He'd say about the books Baker Book House published that we wanted people to say, 'I do not just want to read that book; I want to use that book and I need that book.'"

weeks' rest before orders began flooding in. It is said that even Eleanor Roosevelt purchased books from Baker Book House.

The twenty-fifth-anniversary brochure mentioned plans for expansion: "Also in the offing is a major building and expansion program. Tentative plans call for a doubling in area of the headquarters building, giving more adequate space for the retail store, new offices for the publishing division, as well as much-needed additional room and facilities for receiving and shipping."

3 The Growth Years
1965–1986

The late 1960s onward were years of unprecedented growth for Christian publishing in general and for Baker Book House specifically. The bookstore on Wealthy Street became a gathering place for area pastors, teachers, and laypeople eager to find the newest books or to fill holes in their libraries.

Mondays were often the busiest day because pastors, on their day off, visited the bookstore to meet fellow ministers, discuss and debate theological issues, and soak in the sights and smells of the many books.

Often pastors and teachers visited Grand Rapids just to shop at Baker Book House. The narrow aisles were filled with the likes of D. James Kennedy, Jimmy Swaggart's employees purchasing books for the new seminary library of World Evangelism Bible College, and David Otis Fuller of nearby Wealthy Street Baptist Church. Fuller, whose theology differed from the Reformed tradition of the Dutch Bakers, was known to walk by the store, see a book on display in the window, and step inside to say, "Are you sure you want to sell that book?"

Other visitors included David Martyn Lloyd-Jones, longtime minister at Westminster Chapel in London; Peter Masters, minister at Metropolitan Tabernacle in London; and Ernest E. Jolley, a United Pentecostal Church International minister. Reverend Jolley was one of the rare few given a key to Baker Book House for his twice-yearly visits to the store from his home in Arkansas. He shopped well into the night, leaving his piles of books to be cataloged and billed during the day.

Gary Popma
From Jacketing Books to Operations Manager, Retail Division

When I reflect upon my years at Baker Book House, I am amazed at the success of the company. I am grateful that I had the opportunity to be a small part of that success. I began working for Baker on the day after Labor Day in 1959. My first job was jacketing books, and forty-five years later, in 2004, I retired as operations manager of the retail division. In 1980 the original bookstore on Wealthy Street was moved to the larger and more modern facility on East Paris Avenue. After remodeling and updating, this facility grew to be the premier Christian bookstore in the area.

The used-book department was an interesting place to work. Customers from most states as well as many foreign countries would come to the store and search for scarce theological titles. Pastors on vacation would stop by and browse the shelves for that special book they wanted. It gave us great pleasure to see how excited customers were to own the books they desired.

Working in the retail store gave us opportunity to meet famous authors. One day, Vice President Dan Quayle stopped in the store to autograph his latest book. The line waiting to see him grew so long it became a traffic problem on East Paris Avenue. The vice president signed books for two hours but had to leave in order to make his next stop on time. When he noticed the long line of people waiting to see him, he asked us to pack up a few boxes of his books and he would sign them on the way to the airport. He did so and made a lot of people happy when they finally got a copy of his book.

Colonel Oliver North also made an appearance in the store to sign his latest book. He requested a high reading desk at which he would autograph books. We did not have such a desk, so we had one made. Today, Rich Baker still uses this desk in his office at the store.

J. I. Packer was a guest as well, one time tangling in the leash of a dog that neighborhood children had brought into the store. Harald F. J. Ellingsen, author of the Baker title *Homiletic Thesaurus on the*

Gospels, toppled down the steep steps leading from the used-book section of the store.

Ezra Carter, father of June Carter Cash, bought via mail order *The Preacher's Homiletic Commentary*, a thirty-eight-volume set covering the Old and New Testaments. Gary Popma later saw Carter's son-in-law Johnny Cash at a conference and spoke to him about that commentary series. "I told him that his father-in-law bought that commentary set from Baker Book House. Johnny said, 'Yeah, I have that set now.'"

Building and Buying

Perhaps the biggest move during the 1960s was construction of a twenty-five-thousand-square-foot facility in Ada, just east of Grand Rapids, to house the publishing division and warehouse. The building has been expanded three times since then, adding space to the mailing and warehousing departments as well as publishing-division offices.

> Baker moved its publishing division and warehouse to a new facility in Ada in the 1960s. The building has been expanded three times since then.

From Two-Wheeled Carts to Semitrucks

Shipping protocol has changed dramatically since the Wealthy Street days. When the store first opened, mailing personnel simply stacked packages on a two-wheeled cart and walked the half block to the nearby post office.

Next up was a 1941 Chevy with the backseat removed. Workers stuffed this vehicle to the top, then drove to the Commerce Street post office. Later came a farm truck, which hit the top of the post office overhang because it was too tall.

These days, semitrucks stop at Baker Publishing Group to pick up skids of books destined for accounts. Packaging is mechanized, postage is totaled on computer, and individual books are picked from shelves by workers with scanners strapped on their forearms.

An average of over four hundred large-scale and individual orders—over thirty thousand books—are shipped each day from a warehouse with sixty thousand square feet of space.

Baker Book House completed a twenty-five-thousand-square-foot office and warehouse facility in 1966. Located at 6030 East Fulton Street in Ada, the building has been expanded three times. This is a view of the current complex.

While Baker Book House was expanding its physical space, it was also expanding its space in the publishing realm. In 1968 it acquired the W. A. Wilde Company of Massachusetts, publisher of *Peloubet's Notes* as well as works by distinguished authors such as Bernard Ramm and Wilbur Smith. Wilde also published books of object lessons, Bible quizzes, and puzzles, adding nearly one hundred new titles to the Baker list. Baker also acquired Canon Press, the publishing arm of *Christianity Today*, in 1975.

A section of the new Ada warehouse was hit by a tornado on April 21, 1967. A portion of the roof was blown away, causing considerable damage to the building and the stock inside.

The Evangelical Christian Publishers Association (ECPA) began in 1974 as a member organization for companies involved in the creation and distribution of Christian content around the world. It offered opportunities for networking, sharing information, and advocacy for Christian publishing. Herman Baker made sure Baker Book House was a charter member. Both Richard and Dwight Baker have served on the board of ECPA.

Herman Baker loved the classics of the faith, building his business on the selling of used classics and reprinting the best of the best. He also recognized an opportunity to further expand the business by publishing books for lay readers.

His first venture into reaching this vast market came in 1971 in the form of Ron Hembree's *Fruit of the Spirit*, with a first printing of twenty-five thousand copies. By Baker's fortieth anniversary in 1979, books that reached the general, or trade, market—not pastoral or scholarly works—composed about 60 percent of the Baker list. However, the 1979 catalog of academic books listed over

460 titles on subjects such as biblical studies, theology, apologetics, philosophy, missions, and hymnology.

Baker's complete list ranged from under-one-dollar counseling booklets to multivolume commentaries such as *Barnes' Notes*. Classics appeared in paperback as well as deluxe hardcovers and as part of several series, including Direction Books by contemporary authors and the Summit Series for theological and devotional classics. The list included titles such as *Happiness Is a Choice: A Manual on the Symptoms, Causes, and Cures of Depression* by Frank Minirth and Paul Meier; *Hi! I'm Ann: One Girl's Witness* by Ann Kiemel; *God's Ultimate Purpose: An Exposition of Ephesians 1* by D. Martyn Lloyd-Jones; and *Once Upon a Tree* by Calvin Miller.

Baker Book House was a force in Christian publishing in the 1970s, its influence acknowledged with an article about Herman Baker in the magazine *Publishers Weekly*. The article quoted Herman as saying, "We love to sell a good book. There is no better business to be in. In books we have the richest treasures on earth, the output of the best minds of the ages."

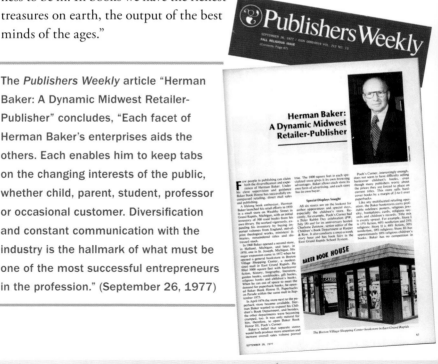

The *Publishers Weekly* article "Herman Baker: A Dynamic Midwest Retailer-Publisher" concludes, "Each facet of Herman Baker's enterprises aids the others. Each enables him to keep tabs on the changing interests of the public, whether child, parent, student, professor or occasional customer. Diversification and constant communication with the industry is the hallmark of what must be one of the most successful entrepreneurs in the profession." (September 26, 1977)

Warren Wiersbe
Author, Pastor, Teacher

I was ten years old in 1939, the year Baker Book House was founded. I was an avid reader and a familiar patron at the public library. A few days before my sixteenth birthday I attended a Youth for Christ rally, heard Billy Graham preach, and gave my heart to Jesus Christ. This decision introduced me to the world of Christian publications. I had no idea that the Lord would call me to serve him as a preacher, teacher, editor, and writer. Now here I am in my mid-eighties having published more than 160 books, forty of them with Baker Publishing Group.

Over the years, I've been in ministry partnerships with ten different Christian publishers. Some of those experiences were shallow and fleeting, others were comfortable but routine, and a few were warmly personal and creative, the kind of relationship that makes you feel like you're part of a happy family. My relationship with Baker has been like the latter.

For one thing, I've been privileged to know the founder and two successive presidents, and they have all known me by name and always made me feel welcome. The founder, Herman Baker, was a dedicated man of integrity whose handshake was as binding as a contract. He may not have totally agreed with everything an author wrote, but if he thought the book had merit, it was published. His son Richard and grandson Dwight have carried on the family traditions beautifully. To these men, publishing first of all means ministry and not business.

My experience at Baker is that the editorial staff respects manuscripts, praises what is good, and makes suggestions for improvements. I hope I never get too old to learn. This is not to say that we have never had our differences, but that our differences never turned into skirmishes that turned into wars. The folks at Baker Publishing Group are professionals. Of course, they have younger employees who are still learning the trade, but I help them catch up on the past and they help me catch up on the present.

I'm grateful for all the Christian publishers who are faithfully ministering today, but right now I'm especially grateful for Baker Publishing Group and all they have done to help their authors minister to people all over the world. Robert Louis Stevenson wrote, "Don't judge each day by the harvest you reap but by the seeds that you plant."

Thank you, Baker Publishing Group, for helping me plant some seeds! One day we shall behold the harvest.

Retail Growth

Baker Book House began as a used-book business and later branched out into publishing. In the 1970s, the retail aspect of the business was going strong under the leadership of Herman Baker's second son, Peter.

The original Holland-area Baker Book House was located downtown on East Eighth Street before moving to Chicago Drive in the Cedar Village Mall.

In 1968 Baker opened a store in Holland, about twenty-five miles southwest of Grand Rapids. A third store opened in 1970 in the Benton Harbor area. Then, between September 1972 and April 1976, three stores opened in Breton Village Mall in Grand Rapids. The first, also named Baker Book House, sold religious and secular titles from the major publishers in both realms. Paperbacks on Parade sold only paperbacks, and the third store, Pooh's Corner, specialized in children's books. In late 1978 the company established an outlet store in Grand Village Mall in the Grand Rapids suburb of Grandville.

The Baker Book House location in Breton Village Mall sold both Christian and secular books. Authors such as Jan Karon, writer of the best-selling Mitford series, visited the store to meet readers and sign books.

The flagship Wealthy Street store continued to sell new books but was the only location that sold used religious books via over-the-counter sales and a robust mail-order business. However, the Wealthy Street store had its idiosyncrasies. While it drew the most learned theologians from churches and colleges across the nation

Pooh's Corner, right, and Paperbacks on Parade sat next to each other in the Breton Village Mall in Grand Rapids. Pooh's Corner, sold by Baker to two of the store's longtime employees, is still in operation today.

Phyllis Bylsma
From Wealthy Street to Ada

I began working for Baker Book House in 1974 in the used-book department at our Wealthy Street location. My boss, Gary Popma, would buy ministers' libraries, and I would type up the purchase quotations for these buys. I recall during my first few weeks that I typed a lengthy quote listing the books we wished to purchase, including the author, title, binding, and price. Before I could send this to our customer, Gary had to check my work. He noticed that I typed "Introduction" as "Intorduction," and he told me I had to retype the entire document. I guess that lesson stayed with me. Today I oversee our data to make sure it is pristine before sending it out electronically to our accounts.

I wore many hats while in retail, including my early role as used-books clerk and then working with Paul Hoeksema in the catalog division, becoming manager when Paul moved to the wholesale division. I was the assistant manager and buyer, plus handled the information-technology needs, when I left the Kentwood store in 1992 to move to the Ada offices.

The days at the Wealthy Street location were memorable because we never knew when we were going to encounter "unexpected guests." Employees parked behind the store and entered via the back door. One day I was talking with Ellen Baker Larson, Rich Baker's sister, when we watched a large rat stroll in the open back door as if he worked there. From that day on, Ellen worked in her cubicle with her feet in a wastebasket.

Moving in 1980 from our home on Wealthy Street to the much-larger bookstore facility on East Paris Avenue was an exciting time. We watched the building turn from a warehouse into a store and were in awe of our classy inventory system for our mail-order business. Numbered bins held our catalog titles; every time a picker grabbed a book, they'd make a note on a blank sticker attached to the bin. Once a week Dawn Baker Faasse and I would "wand the shelves" with our handheld computer. We'd wand the barcode, note how many books had sold that week, and put on a new sticker. An archaic system now, but back then it was top of the line.

I moved from retail to wholesale in March 1992, primarily assisting Rich Baker in sales with various projects and managing the Cambridge Bible line.

I have worked under the leadership of Herman Baker, Richard Baker, and now Dwight Baker, and continue to see growth in staffing, sales, and products. Although much has changed since 1974 and we have grown from a small, family-owned business to a larger, more corporate business, our mission remains the same: "to publish high-quality writings that represent historic Christianity and serve the diverse interests and concerns of evangelical readers." May we continue to follow our mission and do what we love to do: not just sell a book, but change or strengthen a life through the gift of reading.

and the world, it also drew rats that had found a food source at the grocery store located across the street. Longtime employees remember the rats well, along with the epic battles that ensued when one of the rodents made an appearance.

The day finally came when the constraints of space, age, and location meant closing the Wealthy Street store. In July 1980 the move to 2768 East Paris Avenue in the Grand Rapids suburb of Kentwood began. Catalog and office divisions moved first, followed by used books and shipping and receiving, with the store moving last into the remodeled warehouse space of the former Pella Windows store. The space dictated the layout of the building: the Pella offices and showroom at the front of the building remained offices; the warehouse at the back became the retail store.

Employees of Baker Book House Retail Division pose inside the entrance (shown at right) to their new Kentwood, Michigan, store in 1980.

Technology and Business

Baker Book House welcomed technology into the business of selling and publishing books, although at times not as quickly as some employees would have liked. Marilyn Gordon walked in the door for her first day on November 1, 1976; she'd been interviewed off-site so she had never been in the Ada offices before. She admits to a few tears when she discovered there were no electric typewriters in the building.

"I typed 100 words a minute! I didn't know a business would have even one manual typewriter, let alone all manual typewriters," she remembers. Three electric typewriters finally arrived in March 1977. It wasn't long before others saw the benefits of the new technology, and the transition to all electric typewriters was soon complete.

The transition to allowing employees more than one pen at a time took a bit longer. An employee had to request a pen from the business manager, who gave out only one at a time when an empty pen was returned. The legendary Dutch thriftiness that translated into careful business practices continued into the 1990s with the policy of one pen per employee.

The 1980s saw huge strides in computerization. In those days the computer mainframe took up half of a good-sized room. These days it's the size of a shoebox.

The first Macintosh computer arrived in 1987 to manage the author and title index of the complete catalog. Using a Macintosh Plus, employees keyed in information one time and used it many times thereafter. Designer Dan Malda recognized the possibilities for book design as well. Previously, all interior book design was outsourced, but by 1988 all books were typeset on the Mac computers. Soon all art and design work was done on the Mac as well. The change meant a 75 percent reduction in per-page costs and a minimum of a month off the production schedule. What once took weeks from an outside service provider would take just a few days in-house.

"Any time we could demonstrate a need, the Bakers were very open to new technology, programs, and procedures," said Malda, who continues as director of design and typesetting at Baker Publishing Group. "The change allowed me to hire additional staff to handle the volume. The cost savings covered the wages of the employees while maintaining the dramatic reduction in per-page cost."

4 The Transition Years
1987–1999

Herman Baker was a constant presence at Baker Book House from the beginning in 1939 until his retirement in 1987. He took an active role in running the business and as a caretaker of the evangelical, Reformed tradition. He cared deeply about the employees, calling each by name. In fact, after his retirement he continued coming to work every day except for the several weeks he and his wife, Angeline, spent in Florida each year.

"Mr. Baker was always a real gentleman. He always called each employee by name." —Paul Hoeksema

"Mr. B had an uncanny sense of the market—he knew what to reprint and saw trends based on used books and reprints." —Phyllis Bylsma

"My grandfather was elegant, dignified, and reserved, yet kindly. He was the subject of awe and respect, but he was never imperious." —Dwight Baker

"Grandpa had a gentle demeanor and was soft spoken. He said to me, 'Once you find your passion, pursue it.'" —Dave Baker

"Mr. Baker would ask me, 'What are you working on, Marilyn?' And he was innovative for employees. He implemented allowing Friday afternoons off in the summer—we made up the time during the week of course—and allowed us to leave early on the day before a holiday, if we had made up the time earlier." —Marilyn Gordon

"He was always just 'Grandpa' to me. He was engaged in all of our lives and took an interest in what we were doing." —Dan Baker

"Boy, could he pack books! There was never any rattle in a box Mr. Baker packed. He was patient with me, a good mentor, and a smart guy." —Gary Popma

"We got a lot of work done, but we had a lot of fun. It was really a family-owned business; we knew everybody's family." —Marv Moll

"Ben Veldkamp had had a heart attack and I was filling in; I was wracking my brain trying to figure out how to keep things going. The night before my family and I left for vacation, Herm stopped by my office and said, 'I know you're working hard here, so take your family out to dinner.' And he handed me fifty dollars." —Wes Brower

Richard Baker, Herman's oldest son, became president of Baker Book House upon Herman's retirement. Peter Baker, Rich's younger brother, was vice president of the retail sales division at that time as well. Despite his retirement at age seventy-six, Herman continued to play a role in the book business as publisher-at-large. He continued working until his death in February 1991 at age seventy-nine. He died doing what he loved: sitting in his chair listening to classical music at his vacation home in Stuart, Florida. His wife, Angeline, died at age ninety-one in late 2003.

Herman and Richard Baker

Dawn Baker Faasse
Remembers

Dawn Baker Faasse, oldest of Rich and Fran's four children, remembers her grandparents well. She started working at the bookstore in Breton Village Mall when she was sixteen or seventeen, then moved to the Kentwood location. She worked until she had her first child, then went back part-time at Pooh's Corner after a decade. She continued to work at Pooh's after its sale to the current owners. Dawn remarked, "I like to say that I was sold with the store."

Her memories go back to her childhood: "When my mother was in the hospital having Dwight, I stayed with Grandpa and Grandma Baker. Grandma took me to the Wealthy Street store and said, 'Let's press our noses against Grandpa's window and make funny faces at him.' Except that Grandpa was in his office with our minister, Rev. Boomsma. Grandma was mortified!

"There was also the time when Grandpa came home for lunch, as he did every day. Grandma had a steak in the oven for his lunch, but it caught fire. She called the fire department and explained but asked them to send a car instead of the fire trucks. They sent two big fire trucks. Grandpa got home and saw the hullabaloo, but he saw that Grandma was safe outside so he drove right past and went back to work. His life with Grandma was never dull. She was the perfect zany counterpart to his quiet dignity."

Dawn also remembers going to the Wealthy Street store on Sunday afternoons, when it was closed of course, with her dad and her brother Dwight. There was a tiny break room at the foot of the creaky narrow staircase leading up to the used-book department. She and Dwight would head right to the fascinating water cooler and fill the pointy paper cups over and over.

Now she meets with her dad and brothers four times a year for a shareholders' meeting, and afterward they head to Brick Road Pizza, located at the site of the original store. "I always pick the booth where the Nancy Drew books used to be because it was my favorite spot."

Dave Baker

Remembers

Dave Baker represents the Baker family at the retail store. His responsibilities, which include working with school accounts, software, and diversity initiatives, demonstrate his broad view of the role of bookstores in the community.

Dave is the third child and second son of Rich and Fran Baker. He spent his early years working in the family business, first during the summers at the Ada warehouse and later at the bargain bookstore at Grand Village Mall. After graduating from Central Michigan University in 1997, he began work in the printing business. Then in 1999 he started full-time at the Kentwood store.

"I don't think my grandfather knew what he set in motion when he opened his door for business," Dave said. "The company and the family allow individuals to be part of something bigger."

Dave remembers visiting the Breton Village trio of stores regularly with his dad. "After dinner Dad would take Dan and me to the stores to get us out of the house," he said with a laugh. That tradition continues with his own boys: "When I asked one of them what he wanted to do when he grew up, he said, 'I want to be a Baker Book House worker!'"

Dave's interests are in retail and being actively engaged in the community. He draws inspiration from Jean Vanier's words, "A growing community must integrate three elements: a life of silent prayer, a life of service and above all of listening to the poor, and a community life through which all its members can grow in their own gift." Dave notes that "at the store we work to build a healthy community by promoting diversity and inclusion and advocating for those with disabilities." Dave enjoys visiting schools to talk about diversity and to read to students. "Sometimes," he says, "they even listen."

Richard Baker worked his way up the ranks of Baker Book House, from sweeping floors as a boy, to the sales department as a young man, and finally to president at a time of growth and transition for the company. He and his wife, Fran, whom he met at Calvin College and married in 1957, have four children: Dawn Baker

Fleming H. Revell Company

The Fleming H. Revell Company traces its origins to Dwight Lyman Moody, one of the world's most famous evangelists. Moody convinced his brother-in-law, Fleming H. Revell, to take over *Everybody's Paper*, a publication Moody had established in 1867 for use in his beloved Sunday schools.

The Chicago fire of 1871 destroyed Revell's offices and forced him to reconsider his priorities. He began publishing books, which eventually eclipsed Moody's Sunday school papers. The first book in the Revell line was *Grace and Truth under Twelve Different Aspects* by W. P. Mackay. Revell soon became the exclusive publisher of Moody's books, including *Twelve Select Sermons*, which sold 120,000 copies in 1880 alone. Revell would publish thirty of Moody's books plus a biography written by Moody's son Will after Dwight Moody's death in 1899.

Other early authors included R. A. Torrey, Henry Drummond, Hannah Whitall Smith, Charles Gordon (author of Revell's first novel, *The Sky Pilot*), G. Campbell Morgan, E. M. Bounds, William Jennings Bryan, and Harry Emerson Fosdick.

William Barbour, Revell's nephew, became president in 1931 and was succeeded by his son and namesake after he served in World War II. Among the most popular Revell books at the time was *Mr. Jones, Meet the Master*, sermons and prayers of Peter Marshall compiled by his wife Catherine Marshall.

Subsequent bestsellers included *The Total Woman* (1973) by Marabel Morgan and *The Terminal Generation* (1976) by Hal Lindsey. Revell also published books by Elisabeth Elliot, Francis and Edith Schaeffer, and Helen Steiner Rice.

Scott, Foresman and Company purchased Revell in 1978 but in 1982 sold it to Zondervan. Zondervan sold it in 1986 to Guideposts Association, which also created Wynwood Press, the press that published John Grisham's first book, *A Time to Kill*. The contract for Grisham's book resides in the Baker Publishing Group offices, along with handwritten contracts signed by Fleming H. Revell himself. After a string of owners, Revell finally found its real home with Baker Publishing Group.

Faasse, Dwight, David, and Dan. Rich made sure the children were familiar with the company, often bringing them in to the office or warehouse on the weekends.

Moving into Trade Publishing

Richard Baker could see a need in the area of trade publishing. The man who stepped into his father's shoes put his mark on Baker Book House by expanding the company through several key purchases that filled that need. The first, in 1992, was the purchase of the Fleming H. Revell Company and Chosen Books, both based in Tarrytown, New York. Herman Baker had reprinted many books first published by Revell, so he had developed an understanding of its strengths.

Baker Book House acquired Revell's and Chosen's inventory and publishing rights as well as several of their imprints. Rich Baker retained two key Revell staff members—editorial director William Petersen and marketing manager John Topliff—and began publishing Revell and Chosen books from the Grand Rapids offices.

Lonnie Hull DuPont joined the Revell staff in March 1999, having worked for a number of publishers, including Guideposts, and in business for herself in San Francisco. She eventually became editorial director for Revell and is now an acquisitions editor.

"At the time Baker bought Revell, I thought it was an odd fit. But they were good stewards of their resources, and they knew what they were doing," DuPont said. "We're still publishing the books they bought and still repurposing those books that came with Revell."

Today Revell publishes about one hundred books a year, divided between fiction and nonfiction. Jennifer Leep, current editorial director of Revell, credits the 2004 release of *90 Minutes in Heaven* by Don Piper with Cecil Murphey with returning the division

William J. Petersen
Revell Finds a Permanent Home

I was surprised when I saw Rich Baker walk into the Revell offices in Tarrytown, New York, in 1992. I knew that Revell was on the market, but I didn't know why Baker Book House would be interested in buying it.

Baker's interest surprised me because I knew the company to be conservative, not just in theology but also in business. Revell, practically the same size as Baker, was known to take risks in publishing. Although Revell had a strong backlist, it had become known as a frontlist publisher. It seemed to have more of a desire than Baker to hit the bestseller lists. Theologically, Baker drew most of its authors from Calvinistic backgrounds; Revell's authors represented many evangelical streams. And Revell was developing a line of Christian novels, while Baker concentrated on nonfiction.

In addition, Revell was accompanied by Chosen Books, a division that emphasized the Holy Spirit at work today. So it seemed to me that Revell and Chosen would be a very risky—if not foolhardy—venture for a conservative publisher like Baker Book House. And I was sure that Rich Baker would have second thoughts after considering it more carefully.

A few weeks later, however, I was even more surprised when the deal was announced. It wasn't clear at first whether Revell would keep its separate identity or would be merged completely under the Baker imprint. After all, this kind of corporate takeover was new in Christian publishing. In previous business purchases, the publisher that was purchased soon lost its identity as it merged into the larger firm.

But Rich Baker decided to do things differently with Revell and Chosen. While the business operations would be merged completely, editorial acquisitions and development would be independent, though working under Baker editorial vice president Allan Fisher. So Revell and Chosen continued to maintain their separate identities but with a more stable management. Revell authors such as Kevin Leman, Florence Littauer, and Helen Steiner Rice moved the company into a stronger marketing position in Christian publishing.

The bold steps taken by Rich Baker in the 1990s advanced the kingdom and also paid off for the company. In those transitional years, Baker became the major player in Christian publishing it is today.

Chosen Books

Chosen Books was launched in 1970 by four popular writers: John and Elizabeth Sherrill and Leonard and Catherine Marshall LeSourd. Previously the Sherrills had written the bestsellers *The Cross and the Switchblade* with David Wilkerson and *God's Smuggler* with Brother Andrew. Leonard LeSourd was editor of the magazine *Guideposts*, and wife Catherine was author of *A Man Called Peter*, *Beyond Our Selves*, and *Christy*.

But the infant company had no books. The most obvious first title was the Sherrills' current unpublished project. The manuscript was ready, but it was under contract to World Publishing Company. That publisher allowed the Sherrills to buy back the rights and publish it in 1971. *The Hiding Place* by Corrie ten Boom with John and Elizabeth Sherrill—the account of courage and forgiveness in war-torn Holland and Hitler's concentration camps—went on to become a bestseller.

A small staff gradually assembled in a former schoolhouse just down the road from the LeSourds' Evergreen Farm in Lincoln, Virginia. One of those early employees was Jane Campbell, who continues today as editorial director, a job she was appointed to in 1984.

After distribution arrangements with several companies, Chosen Books was sold to Zondervan in the winter of 1982–1983, then sold in 1986, along with Revell, to Guideposts Association. Its permanent home became Baker Publishing Group in 1992.

to a prominent place on the *New York Times* bestseller list for the first time in decades. Leep admits, "We believed *90 Minutes* might sell well but to be honest never predicted it would sell over five million copies."

Jane Campbell

Blessings for Chosen Books

I found it hard to imagine at first that the acquisition of Chosen Books by Baker Publishing Group was anything but a mismatch. A large, family-owned publisher excelling in academic books, many from a Reformed perspective, purchasing a small house, barely twenty-one years old, specializing in books about Spirit-empowered living?

One of my first responses was to suggest that Chosen find another buyer. It was not to be.

What to do, then, but introduce Chosen's titles, present and past, to the new team members and sales reps with gusto and trust God for a bright future.

Gradually the possibilities began to look more possible. At a sales meeting two years after Chosen's purchase, I presented a book about the power of the Spirit, written by a pair of Reformed charismatic authors. After the presentation, Rich Baker urged me to consider increasing the size of Chosen's list. It was welcome affirmation.

The list has increased in size several times in the two decades since, and book distribution along with it. Not even when Chosen was independent—prior to 1983 and housed in the former Quaker schoolhouse—has Chosen ever enjoyed such editorial, marketing, and sales support.

It cannot fail to move me that, in his sovereignty, God ordained the purchase of the small charismatic house by the large Reformed publisher—where a portrait of John Calvin once hung in a hallway—and that he would bless his choice abundantly.

Revell's growth remains steady and its future bright thanks to a core group of authors and its stable team. "We have been working together for a long time and work hard at building strong relationships with authors," Leep said. "We want Revell to feel like home for our authors. And there is something unique and special about this publishing family we've created."

Allan Fisher

Keeping with Academic Tradition

Baker Publishing Group—from the first book Herman Baker published to today—has taken great pains to produce top academic books that dig deep into the rich history of Christian scholarship. I am honored to have been part of that academic tradition for more than twenty years.

When we first learned around 1990 that Moody Press had pulled the plug on its ambitious Wycliffe Exegetical Commentary on the Bible (WEC), we moved rapidly to secure rights to the New Testament portion. Moisés Silva, New Testament editor of the WEC, appeared relieved that Baker had a keen interest in his part of the series, which we eventually titled the Baker Exegetical Commentary on the New Testament (BECNT) and of which he agreed to serve as general editor.

We kept some authors whom Moody had signed but elected to reassign other books. Jim Weaver, who oversaw our academic line during the 1990s, collaborated with Silva to attract just the right authors.

The first BECNT volume was a revised edition of Silva's *Philippians* (1992). The next were Darrell Bock's two volumes on Luke (1994, 1996). With the volumes by Silva and Bock, BECNT was off and running and continues today under the editorship of Robert Yarbrough and Robert Stein. The latest BECNT release is *Galatians* by Douglas J. Moo, professor of New Testament at Wheaton College Graduate School.

The most innovative project we tackled during the 1990s was the Encountering Biblical Studies series. Edited by Walter Elwell, this series helped to upgrade the textbooks used in biblical studies courses in Christian colleges. Working with Elwell on this series, as well as on the Baker Reference Library, was a highlight of my years at Baker.

As the decade neared its end, we stood on the verge of releasing a revised edition of J. Gresham Machen's *New Testament Greek for Beginners*, a coup for Baker. We could do this because the copyright to this classic textbook, long published by Macmillan, would expire in 1999. Many other copyrights would also expire then, of course, including the one protecting Mickey Mouse. Vigorous lobbying by Disney and other media conglomerates resulted in the Sonny Bono Copyright Term Extension Act, which took effect in October 1998. Our plans for Machen's book were foiled by a mouse!

Emphasis on Academics

Despite the acquisition of a number of imprints that propelled Baker Book House deep into the popular Christian market, its emphasis on academic books remained strong. The company's fiftieth anniversary in 1989 was celebrated in part with the publication of the two-volume *Baker Encyclopedia of the Bible*, a monumental work of 2,207 pages edited by Dr. Walter Elwell, professor and dean of the graduate school at Wheaton College.

Elwell's *Encyclopedia* was indicative of Baker's solid commitment to reference works. Similar titles included the *Baker Encyclopedia of Psychology* (1985), edited by David Benner, and the *Evangelical Commentary on the Bible*, edited by Elwell and also released in 1989.

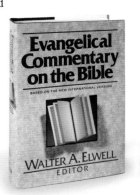 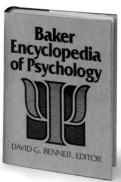

In 1989 Baker published about fifty new academic titles, which were featured in a semiannual catalog and were often sold in college and seminary bookstores. Authors included D. A. Carson, Walter Kaiser, David Hesselgrave, Mark Noll, and many others. College- and seminary-level textbooks covered numerous topics in the fields of theology, preaching, missions, philosophy, economics, and political science. By the late 1980s, psychology texts had become a specialty.

Allan Fisher was a key player in Baker's academic book subculture, first as acquisitions editor for reference and academic books and later as director of publications until 1999.

The emphasis on academic books continues today with series such as The Church and Postmodern Culture, Baker Commentary on the Old Testament, and Engaging Culture. Individual books include

Doug Gunden
Sales Representative

The decade of the 1990s involved rapid change as Baker aggressively pursued new authors and began moving into the digital age. Christian bookstores were a primary market, so most sales trips were made by car as we presented Baker's Sample Plan, which auto-shipped one copy of each new book at its release. Bookstore buyers who would add copies to the plan and place orders for backlist books often said, "If I sold it, replace it." One of the most popular specials was the Baker's Dozen, offering a free copy for every twelve purchased. Other promotions offering increased discounts and free freight helped stores increase margins as chains and special markets became more common and created tension for booksellers.

CBA summer conventions and winter regional events were order-writing shows, and we displayed hundreds of books at these events. Seated at a desk all day with customers waiting to place orders was laborious and time-consuming because orders were handwritten. At one such event, a salesperson left two days' worth of orders in his hotel room and upon his return noted their absence; the maid had apparently discarded them. The conscientious salesperson told Rich Baker what had happened and began the process of contacting as many customers as he could remember and asking for copies of their order. However, another option remained. After an evening of dumpster diving at the rear of a large Dallas hotel in one-hundred-degree heat, he discovered the orders after spotting the words "Baker Book House" showing through a white trash bag. The salesperson, now long retired, recalls the experience as "the worst day of my life!"

Rich Baker was always present at these conventions; he encouraged us and frequently asked what sort of day we had. One time I held up a stack of orders that he estimated to be five or six pounds. He proclaimed, "Pounds of orders, good day!" Thirty or forty orders per day per salesperson was common at those trade shows.

Obviously things have changed and continue to evolve, but the one constant has been the mission of Baker Publishing Group and the Baker family. Their reputation is second to none and they continue a tradition of crafting fine books and placing value in people. I consider it a privilege to have been part of their story.

Old Testament Theology by R. W. L. Moberly, *Understanding Christian Mission* by Scott Sunquist, and *Journey toward Justice* by Nicholas Wolterstorff. The current academic catalog has forty-six pages' worth of new or updated titles and lists hundreds of backlist titles.

Expanding the Baker Vision

The 1980s and 1990s were years of growth, success, and vision for Baker Book House. Regional sales representatives were crisscrossing the nation meeting with bookstores and educational institutions, Baker Book House became the first complete line taken on by Spring Arbor Distributors, and foreign distributors put books into the hands of the world, from Canada to South Africa to Australia. Bestsellers in the late 1980s included Precious Moments books, which sold nearly one million total copies; Louis Caldwell's graduation book *After the Tassel Is Moved*, which approached one million copies sold by 1990; and *Happiness Is a Choice* by Frank Minirth and Paul Meier, which had sold nearly five hundred thousand copies by 1990.

Technology was also making its mark on the world and on Baker Book House. The first desktop computers were being used, fax machines showed up at the office, and eventually the internet and email revolutionized communications, marketing, and electronic access to Baker products. Computers became smaller as their necessity in the workplace grew exponentially.

Changing Identity

Baker Book House began the decade of the 1990s with one identity and exited with another, according to president Dwight Baker. Rich Baker's purchase of Revell and Chosen in 1992 set the company on track as a trade publisher, but it was hard to reeducate the public.

Paul Engle
Nine Years during the Nineties

The years from 1990 to 1999 were a time of major transitions. Perhaps the most dramatic transitions came in the area of technology.

One day I received a book proposal from an East Coast professor that I decided to take a chance on and recommend for publication. Thankfully Al Fisher and Rich Baker agreed. It was released as *The Christian Cyberspace Companion*. This was bleeding edge stuff—most people hadn't even heard of the internet. Even though the term *cyberspace* had a short shelf life, the idea of the internet didn't. The author of this new book, Jason Baker, offered to help set up and host a temporary website for Baker Books. This was March 1995. We ended up, as far as I can tell, being the first CBA publisher to have an operating website. We were soon followed by Nelson, Tyndale, and Zondervan.

By early January 1996 I submitted a recommendation to Rich and Dwight Baker to move ahead full steam and develop our temporary website into a full-fledged operating site. And the rest is history. Jason Baker had been telling me that one day the internet would be as common and transparent as the telephone. That was hard to believe in the days of requisite HTML programming and slow dial-up access.

During this era of technological transition, another development would change the face of publishing. We started seeing Bible computing companies pop up who were asking to license our academic and reference materials and make our titles available to customers electronically. After interviewing and researching a number of companies, we decided to cast our lot with a small company on Whidbey Island in Washington called Logos. That proved to be a wise choice because many of the other companies have since disappeared.

Baker was one of the first major CBA publishers to work with Logos. They helped us develop several boxed library packages of our titles under the name Baker Bytes. We released these at the pivotal time when software was shifting from 5.25-inch to 3.5-inch floppy disks, and we chose this later media, suspecting that eventually the industry would move to online software downloads. But our foot was in the door as one of the first CBA publishers to offer software versions of its titles.

> If we had taken a snapshot of Baker Books in 1990 and then again in 1999, we would have seen a dramatic contrast viewing them side by side. By God's grace Baker kept up with the changes in technology, publishing, and the church to continue its mission of serving the church and its leaders. What a joy and privilege to have had a small part in working alongside many others to navigate the transitions.

"Isn't Baker the company that does classics and reprints?" many asked. "The perception of Baker as a dusty corner of the book business stuck to us for years," according to Dwight. "Of course, Baker did remain a publisher of classics. It was good business to continue working in that area as we established ourselves in the new markets of the late 1990s and the new millennium.

"In fact, we turned the final page on the history only recently. The last carton of Calvin's *Commentaries* shipped from our warehouse in April 2013. The occasion passed without notice or fanfare, but that shipment marked the end of an era for our publishing program. Today our catalog represents only works that we introduce."

New Leadership

The 1990s were also a time of transition in leadership. Rich Baker, who had led the company since 1987, stepped down in 1997, and his oldest son, Dwight, stepped in. Dwight had grown up at the

Rich and Dwight Baker in 2001

company his grandfather started. Like his father, Dwight started out sweeping floors, washing windows, and packing books into boxes in the mailroom.

After graduating from Grand Rapids Christian High School, Dwight attended Calvin College and majored in art. He joined Baker Book House in 1979, was appointed art director in 1983, and became executive vice president in 1991. Dwight designed about half of the company's book covers and jackets, while Dan Malda designed the interior pages of almost all books.

"My dad retired on the last day of a five-year paydown after the purchase of Revell. He took us through the five years of higher risk, then retired and left me with money to invest. We invested in staff, infrastructure, and authors," Dwight said.

But Dwight faced a transition in editorial leadership in 1999 that left the company understaffed and anxious about the future, not to mention facing a serious loss of momentum. Dwight and the leadership team decided that Don Stephenson was the perfect person to lead the editorial department, but Don was in faraway San Diego and not inclined to move to chilly, snowy Michigan. Talks with Don continued over the spring and summer of 1999.

"Employees would ask me about plan B, an alternative should our negotiations with Don fall through," Dwight said. "I didn't have the heart to explain that I had no backup idea. Plan A was it."

Stephenson, however, had his own plans. He and two others—Rodney Clapp and Bobbi Jo Heyboer—dreamed of starting Brazos Press, a line they hoped would publish thoughtful, theologically sound books by leading Christian thinkers from across traditions. Dwight solved all of their problems by hiring all three and bringing Brazos Press under the umbrella of Baker Publishing Group. Dwight liked their ambitions, calling them timely and relevant.

Baker Academic and Brazos Press

Brazos Press gets its name from legend. The story goes that Spanish explorers christened a prominent southwestern river *Los Brazos de Dios* ("the arms of God") when they saw how its winding waters sustained fertile soil in an otherwise dry land. To the explorers, the life-giving river signified the open, inviting embrace of God. Brazos Press seeks to be faithful to this same wide and deep embrace, publishing excellent and accessible works by leading thinkers on topics such as the arts, culture, spirituality, ethics, and theology.

Lauren Winner's *Real Sex: The Naked Truth about Chastity* was a groundbreaking title, as was Jim Wallis's *On God's Side*. Other titles that reflect Brazos's eclectic list include the Brazos Theological Commentary on the Bible series; *Living Worship: A Multimedia Resource for Students and Leaders*; and *iGods: How Technology Shapes Our Spiritual and Social Lives* by Craig Detweiler.

"Lauren Winner's book sold about fifty thousand copies and symbolized what Brazos does: find interesting people not easily classified with traditional labels," said Jim Kinney, associate publisher and editorial director of Baker Academic and Brazos Press. "We love finding voices that people want to pay attention to, then circulating their ideas as broadly as possible."

Kinney sees a bright future for Brazos Press. "We'll continue to be a place where interesting and challenging voices from across the Christian spectrum can find a platform."

Baker Academic serves the academy and the church by publishing books that reflect historic Christianity and its contemporary expressions. Its goal is to produce books notable for their quality and deemed essential reading by students and scholars. "Baker Academic is a tortoise that keeps plodding along providing real stability for the company," Kinney said.

That stability is part of the legacy of Herman Baker in providing useful, thoughtful resources to the academic and church worlds. "We feel very much like we're shepherding a legacy of seventy-five years and helping it transition to the next seventy-five years," Kinney said.

Don Stephenson
One Book, Three Generations

Dwight Baker had a couple of years as president of Baker Publishing Group under his belt when I arrived in October 1999 to oversee the editorial division. That first year might be best described as managed chaos, but after a year we had systems in place to carry us well into the future.

A couple of years after that transitional year, I got a call from Dr. Neil Lightfoot, author of the Baker title *How We Got the Bible*. He said he was sending in another manuscript on the same topic to review for publication. As I waited for the manuscript, I found a copy of the original book and started reading. I was immediately struck with the quality of the material. I was amazed that the book was nearly forty years old. After I finished, I tried to place it in historical context. *How We Got the Bible* was launched in Herman's presidency, transitioned into Rich's presidency, and was still hanging on as Dwight took the reins. It was selling only about a thousand copies a year, but at least it had endured all this time. And that told me Baker published for the long haul.

When I received Dr. Lightfoot's manuscript, I could immediately see that the material should have been a part of the original book. It didn't take a lot of creative insight to see that we should expand and revise the original book with this new material, so I called Dr. Lightfoot. Not only did he like the idea, he was also willing to do a complete revision of the original material. The final book was nearly twice as large as the original.

The design team gave the book a handsome cover and beautiful interior design. The result was the 2003 release of the fortieth-anniversary edition of *How We Got the Bible*. The marketing and sales team gave the book a new launch, and the book really took off.

My tenure at Baker was marked by tremendous change and growth. While Rich acquired Revell and Chosen in the 1990s, Dwight acquired Bethany House during my years at Baker. We broadened our name from Baker Book House Company to Baker Publishing Group. We watched in awe as books topped the *New York Times* bestseller lists. Sales more than doubled. And I am so very grateful to have been part of those events. But when I think back on my time at Baker, I think fondly of *How We Got the Bible* because this one book allowed me the privilege of standing beside three generations of Bakers to help give life to the written word. And for that, I am truly humbled.

Clapp came to Baker as editorial director of Brazos and Heyboer as director of marketing for Baker Academic and Brazos. Brazos was officially launched in 1999, with three books released during its first season in the fall of 2000.

"When Don called me to accept the job, I headed down the hall to spread the good news," Dwight recalled. "My first conversation was with two academic editors who at that very moment were holding a melancholy little conference, as they paged through a newly released academic book and identified all the errors. In fact, the work was so badly edited that we soon withdrew it from the market. Our brief conversation reflected both a low point in our publishing program and the beginning of a turnaround."

During the summer of 1999 Paul Engle served as interim publisher, although he had already accepted a job offer elsewhere. "He kept this private to avoid exacerbating my obvious anxiety," Dwight said, "dutifully managing his department until the week Don arrived."

The careers of these two capable men overlapped at Baker Publishing Group for a single afternoon; it was the first surprise Don Stephenson faced upon his arrival, with many others to follow.

"Through it all," Dwight remembers, "I assumed that all the little pieces would just magically come together again, if Don would just show up here and get to work. That's essentially what happened, with a lengthy series of speed bumps along the way."

On the retail side of the company, all stores except the Kentwood location eventually closed. Then in 1996, Baker Book House experienced a devastating loss when Peter Baker, vice president of retail sales, passed away from leukemia. He was fifty-two years old and left behind his wife, Carol, and four children. Peter was Herman Baker's second son and a visionary in book retailing, one of the first to open a bookstore, Pooh's Corner, devoted exclusively to children's books.

One of the key changes made during this time reflected the growth and breadth of Herman Baker's vision and Richard Baker's forward thinking. The publishing divisions began operating under the name Baker Publishing Group, though the name Baker Book House Company survives as the official name of the organization. The bookstore in Kentwood kept the Baker Book House moniker, a reflection of the original name given so long ago to a small bookstore that sold used books.

BAKER PUBLISHING GROUP

5 The New Millennium
2000–Present

The early years of the new millennium saw Baker Publishing Group expanding once again, this time nearly doubling the line and strengthening exponentially its reach into the fiction market with the purchase of Bethany House Publishers. Bethany House, based in Bloomington, Minnesota, is well known for its deep historical fiction line, contemporary and Amish fiction, and vibrant nonfiction line. Its authors include Beverly Lewis, Lynn Austin, Julie Klassen, Tracie Peterson, Dee Henderson, Albert Mohler, Dr. William Marty, Stephen M. Miller, Jack Graham, and a host of other award-winning novelists and nonfiction writers.

Jim Parrish started at Bethany House in 1984 in sales and customer service, eventually becoming business manager and vice president. In 2008 he became executive vice president and director when Gary Johnson stepped aside as president of the division.

"When we were informed that Bethany Fellowship was planning to sell the publishing house, we were shaken by the idea that a New York publisher or conglomerate might purchase Bethany House and promptly break the company apart, reorganize, consolidate, let most of our staff go, and eventually lose the distinctive character of Bethany House," said Parrish, who also leads Chosen Books. "But when we heard the buyer was Baker, we were greatly relieved. We knew Baker to be a strong and stable presence in the publishing world. And, under Baker, Bethany House, like the other Baker divisions, continues to develop its own unique focus and identity to meet the needs of the authors we partner with and the readers we serve."

Dave Horton, vice president of editorial for Bethany House, agrees. "We had gotten to know their president at the time, Rich Baker, over the years, and anyone who has had interaction with the Baker family has found it to be a positive experience. That added a layer of comfort, knowing we would be working with these good people."

Parrish had served with Rich Baker on a CBA board in the late 1980s and early 1990s. "I appreciated Rich's no-nonsense get-the-job-done attitude. I also became aware of his personal interest in getting books overseas. He was willing to make sacrifices to see that Baker books serve the needs of readers far outside our borders."

For Horton, a chance meeting at the Baker CBA booth spoke volumes about Rich Baker and the Baker family: "I complimented him on a Baker book I had read; he told me that if I was interested in any other Baker titles to give him a call and he'd send it. Six months later I did just that. The book was sitting on my desk the next day. He was serious about people reading his books."

That respect continues under the leadership of Rich's son Dwight Baker. "He's thoughtful and thought-provoking, confident and decisive," Horton said. "We can get an answer within minutes to a question that could take a board or committee days or weeks to work on. And he's humble enough to take the blame if a decision goes awry. That is an admirable trait."

The purchase of Bethany House Publishers ramped up Baker Publishing Group to another level, expanding its reach and its product lines. In 2007, Don Stephenson retired, replaced by Jack Kuhatschek as executive vice president and publisher. Kuhatschek

Gary and Carol Johnson were vital to the growth of Bethany House Publishers from 1960 until they stepped aside from their leadership roles in 2008.

Bethany House Publishers

Bethany House Publishers grew out of Bethany Fellowship, a small community dedicated to training, sending, and supporting missionaries. Bethany Fellowship began in 1945 when five young families sold their homes and pooled their resources to buy a common residence in Minneapolis they called Bethany House. These families devoted all they had to training young people to take the gospel to the world. As the organization expanded, they bought a large farm in Bloomington, Minnesota, where the ministry continues today.

Bethany Fellowship began formally training students when Bethany College of Missions opened in 1948. Later Bethany formed their own sending agency—Bethany Fellowship Ministries. Over the years several thousand Bethany graduates have served God in more than fifty countries.

Bethany House Publishers was birthed in 1956 when Bethany printed its first publication—*The Changing Climate* by Arthur Bloomfield—and over the next several years new pamphlets and books were published. In 1960 Gary Johnson became manager of the campus bookstore at the College of Missions, inheriting also the leadership of the fledgling publishing ministry.

Johnson saw the potential for Bethany's publishing efforts in part thanks to the book *Why Revival Tarries* by Leonard Ravenhill, published in 1959 and still in print with close to one million copies sold. Gary began publishing out-of-print books—by Andrew Murray, Charles Finney, and so on—before finding a larger presence in the marketplace with *The Kingdom of the Cults* by Walter Martin in 1965 and *The Christian Family* by Larry Christenson in 1970.

Under Gary's leadership, Bethany House Publishers became one of the main sources of financial support for all of Bethany Fellowship's ministry operations. Today, Bethany House produces about seventy-five new titles a year, with a backlist of about 1,100 titles. Its books routinely win awards—including Christy Awards, Carol Awards, and others—and have been translated into more than sixty languages.

Gary's wife, Carol, joined him in 1978 as the editorial director after editing part-time for Bethany House in the 1960s. Bethany's fiction program started to take off when Carol acquired Janette Oke's first book, *Love*

Comes Softly, in 1978. Its success came in large part because of Successful Living, a Christian business designed to bring inspirational reading directly into homes, grocery stores, drugstores, and other general-marketplace locations. Women bought *Loves Comes Softly* in droves at the home parties, and this provided an eager audience when the sequel, *Love's Enduring Promise*, followed the next year. Christian bookstores noticed, and the series took off. Oke penned eight books in the original series, plus four more in the Prairie Legacy series that followed. Movies made from the Love Comes Softly series became some of Hallmark Channel's most popular after their release, beginning in 2003.

Carol Johnson was instrumental in starting the Christy Awards in the late 1990s, and she was recently honored when American Christian Fiction Writers renamed their fiction awards the Carol Awards.

After a successful run of children's fiction works, Beverly Lewis was encouraged by a Bethany House editor to write her first full-length novel. That novel—*The Shunning*, published in 1997—launched the hugely popular Amish fiction trend that fills bookstore shelves today.

"Christian retailers came around to the value of fiction because they knew Bethany House was serious about it. CBA retailers feel safe selling Bethany's novels," Gary said.

The Johnsons, along with the Bethany House staff, were hugely relieved to hear that Baker Publishing Group was the house that would be purchasing the company in 2003. Gary had known the founder, Herman Baker, "a true statesman in the Christian publishing world," he said, and had gotten to know Rich Baker through CBA and ECPA. "We knew of Baker's reputation and believed that of any of the companies that could buy us, Baker was most likely to keep Bethany a distinct entity within the corporate whole." That is exactly what happened.

had joined Baker Publishing Group in 2005 as editorial director of the Baker Books division.

"When I came to Baker Publishing Group in 2005, I was very encouraged by the amazing growth the company had experienced in recent years," Kuhatschek said. "I also saw great potential for additional growth and ministry, and I was eager to join the very talented editorial team and to help them move to the next level."

Baker Books

Chad Allen, editorial director of the Baker Books division of Baker Publishing Group, has remarked, "I've stepped in as a character in the larger story and want to play that part well."

Baker Books is a direct descendant of Herman Baker's vision: publishing thoughtful, relevant, and engaging books that challenge readers and the church at large to think and take action. "A keystone of our program is helping the church interact and engage with culture," said Allen, who began at Baker in 2001 as a project editor and became editorial director in 2010.

He cites books such as *The Peacemaker* and *Resolving Everyday Conflict* by Ken Sande and *unChristian* by David Kinnaman and Gabe Lyons as emblematic of what Baker Books is trying to do.

"When people want to know what leading evangelicals are thinking and teaching, we want them to come to Baker Books for those resources."

While the lines occasionally blur between Baker Books, Baker Academic, and Brazos Press—executive editor Bob Hosack acquires for all three, for example—the mission remains the same: a commitment to quality books by top authors on relevant topics.

Bibles

Baker was the exclusive North American distributor of Cambridge Bibles from 1990 to 2014. Cambridge University Press has been publishing Bibles since 1591 and the King James Version since 1629, making it the oldest Bible publisher in the world.

In 2008 Baker purchased the publishing rights to GOD'S WORD Translation (GW), which was produced by a translation committee under the direction of the God's Word to the Nations Mission Society with the goal of accurately translating the Bible from the Hebrew, Aramaic, and Greek texts into clear, everyday English. When it first released in 1995 a distributor was responsible for publishing it, and rights were transferred to a small publisher in Florida in 2003. The bestselling editions at that time included *God's Word for Boys* and *God's Word for Girls*.

By 2008 Baker had a long track record of publishing books, but the acquisition of rights to GW marked its first venture into Bible publishing. Its acquisition was typical of transitions over the history of the company. "The start of Bible publishing got us in over our heads," Dwight Baker said, "which is when we grow and do some of our best work. We have learned that Bible publishing is challenging, but we are learning by actually doing it."

Significant new releases under Baker's care have been the *God Girl Bible* with devotional notes by Hayley DiMarco, *The Names of God Bible* with commentary from Ann Spangler, and the *Pray the Scriptures Bible* with prayers written by Kevin Johnson. Baker has also begun to release new editions of other translations, including the King James Version.

Brian Vos, editorial director for Bible publishing, said, "It's a wonderful responsibility to be able to publish the Bible. We're excited about the success we've had so far and the valuable in-house experience we've gained. We're looking forward to expanding our service in the Bible category."

Recession

The early 2000s—a time of continued growth and deepened commitment to reaching readers with fine books—were the calm before the storm of a huge recession that hit the United States, with Michigan particularly hard hit. Sales in 2008 and 2009 plummeted as consumers struggled to make ends meet due to job loss and higher costs of living. The book publishing industry was hit especially hard, with Baker Publishing Group no exception.

Many other companies went through staff reductions during this time, a step that Dwight Baker sought to avoid. Instead, the company announced in late 2008 that every employee making more than twelve dollars per hour would receive a 5 percent pay cut. This action, in addition to a hiring freeze and many other spending reductions, enabled the company to get through the recession. Staff members' pay was later restored as economic conditions improved.

Office staff also took shifts in the warehouse when the hiring freeze meant warehouse workers were falling behind in processing returns. They donned jeans and T-shirts and got to work opening cartons, putting books back on shelves, and handling damaged books.

"When their backs are against the wall, the Bakers' way has been to take austerity measures," said Chad Allen, who did his shifts in the warehouse. "It was the right thing to do. Dwight demonstrated that there is more to life than money. His priorities are people, books, and community."

The company also banded together to support employees in times of personal crisis. One of these took place in 2009 when the wife of human resources director Dan Baker, youngest son of Richard Baker, was critically injured in a car accident and later died, leaving two children behind. The staff of Baker Publishing Group prayed and provided encouragement and support to one of their own.

Dan Baker

Remembers

Dan Baker began at Baker Publishing Group as his brothers and sister before him: coming into the offices as a young child. "My dad would take me along with him some Saturday mornings," Dan recalled. "While he was in the office working the Dictaphone machine, I would sit at a table in the warehouse and put dust jackets on hardcover books. I got pretty good at it after a while and would like to think that on a nightstand somewhere in the world, there's still a *Good Morning, Lord* devotional with my fingerprints on it."

He worked at one of the bookstores at Breton Village Mall as he grew older, under the leadership of manager Heidi Zophy. "We knew there were other stores in the area larger than us. Heidi worked to distinguish Baker Book House by emphasizing trusted relationships with loyal customers. She expected all of us to do our work with professionalism, grow in our knowledge of the books, be attentive to the order and upkeep of the store, and do a lot of old-fashioned hand selling rooted in a love of the printed word. All of this made an impression on me."

Dan received a BA from St. Olaf College in Minnesota, then returned to Grand Rapids and Baker Book House in 1997 as a marketing assistant. He worked in marketing and sales roles for eleven years while taking night classes to complete a graduate business degree. He transitioned to human resources in 2008 and is now executive vice president of human resources, a role he relishes.

"As we have grown, it's been important to ensure that our employment and management practices are fitting for an organization of our size, while also working to preserve the best of an innovative small-company culture. The contribution I want to make is to foster a work environment where every person feels able to confidently apply their God-given gifts to the life-changing work of Christian publishing and retailing and to find meaning and fulfillment in what they do."

For Wes Brower, executive vice president of finance and operations, the Baker family showed their support and concern when his son Dan was battling leukemia at Northwestern Memorial Hospital in Chicago a number of years ago. The family received many cards and gift baskets and much prayer support through Dan's three-and-a-half-month battle with the disease that took his life.

A number of people at the company had their bone marrow tested—at company expense—to see if they were a match for Dan Brower. None were, but several years later one of those tested matched someone in need. The bone marrow donation was made and was a success.

Looking to the Future

The future is bright for Baker Publishing Group. Baker Book House, the retail arm of the company, recently underwent a million-dollar renovation to update and expand the store. Current best-sellers, backlist titles, and a deep academic section draw casual readers and scholarly experts. Customers come from around the

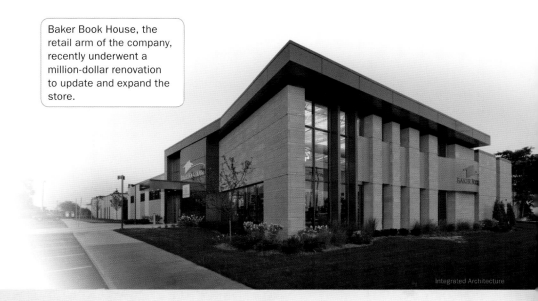

Baker Book House, the retail arm of the company, recently underwent a million-dollar renovation to update and expand the store.

Integrated Architecture

world to shop the store's ninety thousand used books and bargain area; authors—from Ted Dekker to Liz Curtis Higgs to Charles Stanley—are eager to do events at the store; and the community has found a meeting place replete with private conference rooms, Wi-Fi, a café, event space, and comfortable seating.

Broader service to the Christian publishing and retail community remains part of the Baker ethos. It began with Herman Baker playing a key role in the start of CBA and ECPA and continued with Rich Baker's role on the boards of CBA and ECPA. Dwight Baker is part of the ECPA executive committee today, and Sue Smith, store manager of Baker Book House, is chairperson of the CBA board of directors.

Mission Statement
Baker Publishing Group publishes high-quality writings that represent historic Christianity and serve the diverse interests and concerns of evangelical readers.

Baker Publishing Group, always ready to tackle new trends, was on the cutting edge of the ebook revolution in 2008 when *The Pawn* by Steven James and *unChristian* by David Kinnaman and Gabe Lyons became the first Baker Publishing Group ebooks. Between 2008 and 2012 almost all backlist titles were converted to ebook format. The current focus is on frontlist title conversion, with all new titles (300–350 titles a year) released in ebook form to accommodate the habits of twenty-first-century readers. The company has about twenty-five resellers (such as Amazon and Apple) of ebooks in the United States and abroad.

"Sales and profits from digital books have helped us continue publishing with minimal interruption to the company," said Dave Lewis, executive vice president of sales and marketing. "Fiction was the category that exploded for ebook sales first, and the reason we have kept pace with the overall industry in ebook sales."

Lewis credits Nathan Henrion and others in the sales department who were quick to understand the power of promoting certain ebooks at low prices to find new readers.

"We love to experiment with price points, then measure the results and create new promotions based upon the knowledge gained in the process," Lewis said. "We predict that ebooks will become one-third of the total sales of Baker Publishing Group within the next five years."

The publishing company converts most of its titles to ebooks at the Ada offices, using outside vendors only when necessary. Lewis said, "We believe that doing our own conversions creates a more reliable and better-looking ebook."

With an active list of 2,800 titles and an annual output of 270 new works, Baker Publishing Group continues to look to the future. Now in its third generation of Baker family leadership, the company

The company remains family owned. Pictured from left to right are Dan Baker, Dawn Baker Faasse, Rich Baker, Dave Baker, and Dwight Baker.

Board of Directors

Dwight Baker
CEO/President, Baker Book House
Company

Dan Baker
Executive Vice President, Human
Resources, Baker Book House
Company

John Jackoboice
Chairman Emeritus, Monarch
Hydraulics

Bruce Ryskamp
Former President/CEO, Zondervan
Corporation, Retired

Kathryn Scanland
President, Greystone Global

Quentin Schultze
Professor of Communications,
Calvin College

Jody Vanderwel
President, Grand Angels

C. Jeffrey Wright
CEO, Urban Ministries, Inc.

Back row from left to right: Jody Vanderwel, Bruce Ryskamp, Dwight Baker, Quentin Schultze, C. Jeffrey Wright; *front row from left to right:* John Jackoboice, Kathryn Scanland, and Dan Baker

is preparing for the next decades. Dwight Baker created a governing board in September 2012 made up of Dwight and Dan Baker and six nonfamily members. These thoughtful men and women are tasked with guiding the organization into the fourth generation and beyond. And while Dwight leads Baker Book House Company, the ownership of the company is shared among the second and third generations of the Baker family.

Rich Baker sees much to praise at the company his father started and that he piloted for a decade. "There is always a market for books from Baker Publishing Group. We can go along as an independent publisher for years. I'm very optimistic for our immediate future with the position we're in and the grace of God."

Baker Publishing Group looks to the future even as it celebrates the past seventy-five years. The company's goal remains the same, reflecting the words of Herman Baker: "We love to sell a good book. There is no better business to be in."

Note from Dwight Baker

When we review the past few decades, it becomes clear that we have made our greatest progress during those periods when our confidence and comfort levels are comparatively low. I refer to those occasions when we have over-extended ourselves and faced demands that were outside our usual boundaries. The challenge might appear in the form of a business acquisition or an ambitious new project. Or it might arrive in the form of a threat, such as the recession, a large failure, or the departure of a highly valued employee.

The scope of our publishing and retailing services will continue to expand as long as we don't grow too comfortable in our own space. We do our best when we are in over our heads, and we eventually forget about how panicked we felt at the time. That's one of the amazing aspects about book publishing. Yes, it is conservative by nature and rich with tradition, but every morning on the job I still feel like a freshman. There is still so much to learn about serving the church through publishing, and that is its enduring joy.

Employees in 2014

With gratitude for God's faithfulness, we celebrate Baker's seventy-fifth anniversary and the opportunity to serve Christ's kingdom.

Lisa Alder
Katherine Alderink
Chad Allen
Charity Allen
Ruth Anderson
Joseph Arnold
Sharon Asmus
Steven Ayers
Thomas Ayers
Daniel Baker
David Baker
Dwight Baker
Erik Baker
Richard Baker
Michelle Bardin
Barbara Barnes
Robin Barnett
Erin Bartels
Nancy Bashlor
Randy Benbow
Twila Bennett
Brett Benson
Jack Boers
Robert Bol
Kimberly Boldt
Brian Bolger
Kelsalyn Bowen
Christopher Brannon
Jeffrey Braun
Heather Brewer
Kirsten Brink

Patricia Brinks
Wesley Brower
Brian Brunsting
Philip Burgess
Noelle Buss
Deborah Butgereit
Gabrielle Byle
Eric Bylsma
Phyllis Bylsma
Jane Campbell
Nancy Capps
Lauren Carlson
Donna Carpenter
Hannah Carpenter
Carra Carr
Bethany Castleman
Ellen Chalifoux
Lamont Chivis
Brittany Clark
David Clinton
Robert Clinton
Lisa Cockrel
Jeanne Covell
Vicki Crumpton
Bryan Dam
Cathy Davis
Lindsay Davis
Kara Day
Debra Deacon
Donna De For
Maria Delgado

Deborah Denkins
William DeRooy
Brianna DeWitt
James Dodds
Andrea Doering
LaVonne Downing
Lonnie Hull DuPont
Bryan Dyer
Angela Dykhuis
Linda Dykhuis
Christina Dykstra
LaRaye Dykstra
Philip Dykstra
Max Eerdmans
Wanda Elliott
Heather Engel
Jessica English
James Ernest
Kristina Ettema
Melanie Evans
Alex Fane
Kevin Ferguson
Lynne Finkler
Daniel Gerard
Paula Gibson
Rochelle Gloege
Marilyn Gordon
Amy Green
David Greendonner
Amanda Halash
Amanda Hall

Robert Hand
Kathleen Harley
Sara Harlow
Suzanne Harris
Lanette Haskins
Timothy Hausler
Marianne Hay
James Heaton
Staci Heinzelman
Janelle Henderson
Anna Henke
Nathan Henrion
Brittany Higdon
Paul Higdon
Mark Highman
Luke Hinrichs
Erin Hollister
Sandra Hopkins
David Horton
Robert Hosack
Kelly Houghtaling
Jennifer Huber
Dale Huizenga
Scott Hurm
Christine Jager
Michael Jantzen
Rodney Jantzen
Christina Jasko
William Johnston
James Kinney
Rachel Klompmaker
Elizabeth Kool
Kristin Kornoelje
James Korsmo
Janet Kraima
Jack Kuhatschek
Lloydeen La Huis
Celia Larsen
Joel Lawrence
Audrey Leach
Jennifer Leep
David Lewis
David Long
Samantha Lovell

Stephanie Lovell
Hollene Lowetz
Lynnae Lubbers
Shelly MacNaughton
Janelle Mahlmann
Carissa Maki
Daniel Malda
Claudia Marsh
Melissa Marshall
Louis McBride
Lynn McBroom
Trinity McFadden
Andrew McGuire
Jeffery McMullin
Michele Misiak
Mary Molegraaf
Marvin Moll
Joshua Mosey
Donald Mulder
David Nelson
Michelle Niswonger
Rebecca Niswonger
Jennifer Nutter
Betty Nyman
Steven Oates
Lois Oberlin
Jennifer Parker
James Parrish
Charlene Patterson
Laura Peterson
Timothy Peterson
Daniel Pitts
Michelle Plichta
Cassandra Rademaker
Pedro Ramos-Perez
Nancy Renich
Jessica Rickert
Nancy Roersma
Joyce Ross
Maureen Ruge
Jazz Salo
Raela Schoenherr
Karen Schurrer
Bill Shady

Jennifer Shepard
Alicia Sheppard
Amy Sherman
Lanny Sherman
Andrew Sherwood
Matthew Skeens
Mason Slater
Julie Smith
Susan Smith
Steven Speckman
Natasha Sperling
Lindsey Spoolstra
Ashleigh Steele
Karen Steele
Jolene Steffer
Gregory Stevens
Megan Stoutjesdyk
Peter Sweers
Mary Sytsma
Elisa Tally
Robert Teigen
Stacey Theesfield
Reed Turchetti
Wells Turner
Cheryl VanAndel
John VandenAkker
Terri Van Den Berg
Patricia VanderWeide
Aaron Van Duinen
Christine VanHeuvelen
Debra Veenstra
Brian Vos
Eric Walljasper
Jeremy Wells
Mary Wenger
Timothy West
Wendy Wetzel
Kathy Worst
Julie Zahm
Marie Zyskowski
Samuel Zyskowski

Bestsellers

Bestselling Titles

Over One Million

God's Psychiatry, Charles Allen
The Christian Family, Larry Christenson
Born Again, Charles Colson
Free to Be Thin, Neva Coyle and Marie Chapian
Jesus Freaks, dc Talk
Hide or Seek, James Dobson
Little Girls & Little Boys Bible Storybooks, Carolyn Larsen
Making Children Mind without Losing Yours, Kevin Leman
The Shunning, Beverly Lewis
Personality Plus, Florence Littauer
The Helper, Catherine Marshall
Something More, Catherine Marshall
To Live Again, Catherine Marshall
None of These Diseases, S. I. McMillen and David Stern
Love Comes Softly, Janette Oke
Love's Enduring Promise, Janette Oke
Once Upon a Summer, Janette Oke
When Calls the Heart, Janette Oke
Angel Unaware, Dale Evans Rogers
God Calling, A. J. Russell
The Christian's Secret of a Happy Life, Hannah Whitall Smith

Over Two Million

All Things Are Possible through Prayer, Charles Allen
God's Smuggler, Brother Andrew
The Master Plan of Evangelism, Robert Coleman
His Needs, Her Needs, Willard Harley
Beyond Our Selves, Catherine Marshall

The Total Woman, Marabel Morgan
The Cross and the Switchblade, David Wilkerson

Over Five Million

90 Minutes in Heaven, Don Piper
In His Steps, Charles Sheldon
The Hiding Place, Corrie ten Boom

Bestselling Authors

Over One Million

Charles Colson

Hayley DiMarco

James Dobson

Carolyn Larsen

Florence Littauer

S. I. McMillen and David Stern

Hannah Whitall Smith

Warren Wiersbe

Over Two Million

Brother Andrew

Larry Christenson

Robert Coleman

Neva Coyle and Marie Chapian

dc Talk

Elisabeth Elliot

Dave and Neta Jackson

Marabel Morgan

Over Three Million

Willard Harley

T. D. Jakes

Gilbert Morris

Tracie Peterson

Michael Phillips

Dale Evans Rogers

Lauraine Snelling

Over Five Million

Charles Allen

Kevin Leman

Lois Gladys Leppard

Catherine Marshall

Don Piper

Helen Steiner Rice

Charles Sheldon

Corrie ten Boom

David Wilkerson

Over Fifteen Million

Beverly Lewis

Over Twenty-Five Million

Janette Oke